The Human Body

Teacher Supplement

1:1

Answers
IN GENESIS™

GOD'S
DESIGN®

4th Edition
Debbie & Richard Lawrence

God's Design for Life
The Human Body Teacher Supplement

Reprinted July 2020

Fourth edition. Copyright © 2008, 2016 by Debbie & Richard Lawrence

ISBN: 978-1-62691-419-3

Published by Answers in Genesis, 2800 Bullittsburg Church Rd., Petersburg KY 41080

Book designer: Diane King
Editor: Gary Vaterlaus

AnswersInGenesis.org • GodsDesign.com

Welcome to
GOD'S DESIGN®

LIFE

God's Design for Life is a series that has been designed for use in teaching life science to elementary and middle school students. It is divided into three books: *The World of Plants*, *The World of Animals*, and *The Human Body*. Each book has 35 lessons including a final project that ties all of the lessons together.

In addition to the lessons, special features in each book include biographical information on interesting people as well as fun facts to make the subject more fun.

Although this is a complete curriculum, the information included here is just a beginning, so please feel free to add to each lesson as you see fit. A resource guide is included in the appendices to help you find additional information and resources. A list of supplies needed is included at the beginning of each lesson, while a master list of all supplies needed for the entire series can be found in the appendices.

Answer keys for all review questions, worksheets, quizzes, and the final exam are included here. Repro-ducible student worksheets and tests may be found in the digital download that comes with the purchase of the curriculum. You may download these files from GodsDesign.com/Life.

If you prefer the files on a CD-ROM, you can order that from Answers in Genesis at an additional cost by calling 800-778-3390.

If you wish to get through all three books of the *Life* series in one year, plan on covering approximately three lessons per week. The time required for each lesson varies depending on how much additional information you include, but plan on about 40 to 45 minutes.

Quizzes may be given at the conclusion of each unit, and the final exam may be given after lesson 34.

If you wish to cover the material in more depth, you may add additional information and take a longer period of time to cover all the material, or you could choose to do only one or two of the books in the series as a unit study.

Why Teach Life Science?

Maybe you hate science or you just hate teaching it. Maybe you love science but don't quite know how to teach it to your children. Maybe science just doesn't seem as important as some of those other subjects you need to teach. Maybe you need a little moti-vation. If any of these descriptions fits you, then please consider the following.

It is not uncommon to question the need to teach your kids hands-on science in elementary school. We could argue that the knowledge gained in science will be needed later in life in order for your children to be more productive and well-rounded adults. We could argue that teaching your children science also teaches them logical and inductive thinking and reasoning skills, which are tools they will need to be more successful. We could argue that science is a necessity in this technological world in which we live. While all of these arguments are true, not one of them is the real reason that we should teach our children science. The most important reason to teach science in elementary school is to give your children an understanding that God is our Creator, and the Bible can be trusted. Teaching science from a creation perspective is one of the best ways to reinforce your children's faith in God and to help them counter the evolutionary propaganda they face every day.

God is the Master Creator of everything. His handiwork is all around us. Our Great Creator put in place all of the laws of physics, biology, and chemistry. These laws were put here for us to see His wisdom and power. In science, we see the hand of God at work more than in any other subject. Romans 1:20 says, "For since the creation of the world His invisible attributes are clearly seen, being understood by the things that are made, even His eternal power and Godhead, so that they [men] are without excuse." We need to help our children see God as Creator of the world around them so they will be able to recognize God and follow Him.

The study of life science helps us understand the balance of nature so that we can be good stewards of our bodies, the plants, and the animals around us. It helps us appreciate the intricacies of life and the wonders of God's creation. Understanding the world of living things from a biblical point of view will prepare our children to deal with an ecology-obsessed world. It is critical to teach our children the truth of the Bible, how to evaluate the evidence, how to distinguish fact from theory and to realize that the evidence, rightly interpreted, supports biblical creation, not evolution.

It's fun to teach life science! It's interesting, too. Children have a natural curiosity about living things, so you won't have to coax them to explore the world of living creatures. You just have to direct their curiosity and reveal to them how interesting life science can be.

Finally, teaching life science is easy. It's all around us. Everywhere we go, we are surrounded by living things. You won't have to try to find strange materials for experiments or do dangerous things to learn about life.

How Do I Teach Science?

In order to teach any subject you need to understand how people learn. People learn in different ways. Most people, and children in particular, have a dominant or preferred learning style in which they absorb and retain information more easily.

If a student's dominant style is:

Auditory
He needs not only to hear the information but he needs to hear himself say it. This child needs oral presentation as well as oral drill and repetition.

Visual
She needs things she can see. This child responds well to flashcards, pictures, charts, models, etc.

Kinesthetic
He needs active participation. This child remembers best through games, hands-on activities, experiments, and field trips.

Also, some people are more relational while others are more analytical. The relational student needs to know why this subject is important, and how it will affect him personally. The analytical student, however, wants just the facts.

If you are trying to teach more than one student, you will probably have to deal with more than one learning style. Therefore, you need to present your lessons in several different ways so that each student can grasp and retain the information.

Grades 3–8

The first part of each lesson should be completed by all upper elementary and junior high students. This is the main part of the lesson containing a reading section, a hands-on activity that reinforces the ideas in the reading section (blue box), and a review section that provides review questions and application questions.

Grades 6–8

In addition, for middle school/junior high age students, we provide a "Challenge" section that contains more challenging material as well as additional activities and projects for older students (green box).

We have included periodic biographies to help your students appreciate the great men and women who have gone before us in the field of science.

We suggest a threefold approach to each lesson:

Introduce the topic

We give a brief description of the facts. Frequently you will want to add more information than the essentials given in this book. In addition to reading this section aloud (or having older children read it on their own), you may wish to do one or more of the following:

- Read a related book with your students.
- Write things down to help your visual learners.
- Give some history of the subject. We provide some historical sketches to help you, but you may want to add more.
- Ask questions to get your students thinking about the subject.

Make observations and do experiments

- Hands-on projects are suggested for each lesson. This part of each lesson may require help from the teacher.
- Have your students perform the activity by themselves whenever possible.

Review

- The "What did we learn?" section has review questions.
- The "Taking it further" section encourages students to
  - Draw conclusions
  - Make applications of what was learned
  - Add extended information to what was covered in the lesson
- The "FUN FACT" section adds fun or interesting information.

By teaching all three parts of the lesson, you will be presenting the material in a way that children with any learning style can both relate to and remember.

Also, this approach relates directly to the scientific method and will help your students think more scientifically. The *scientific method* is just a way to examine a subject logically and learn from it. Briefly, the steps of the scientific method are:

1. Learn about a topic.
2. Ask a question.
3. Make a hypothesis (a good guess).
4. Design an experiment to test your hypothesis.
5. Observe the experiment and collect data.
6. Draw conclusions. (Does the data support your hypothesis?)

Note: It's okay to have a "wrong hypothesis." That's how we learn. Be sure to help your students understand why they sometimes get a different result than expected.

Our lessons will help your students begin to approach problems in a logical, scientific way.

How Do I Teach Creation vs. Evolution?

We are constantly bombarded by evolutionary ideas about living things in books, movies, museums, and even commercials. These raise many questions: Did dinosaurs really live millions of years ago? Did man evolve from apes? Which came first, Adam and Eve or the cavemen? Where did living things come from in the first place? The Bible answers these questions and this book accepts the historical accuracy of the Bible as written. We believe this is the only way we can teach our children to trust that everything God says is true.

There are five common views of the origins of life and the age of the earth:

Historical biblical account	Progressive creation	Gap theory	Theistic evolution	Naturalistic evolution
Each day of creation in Genesis is a normal day of about 24 hours in length, in which God created everything that exists. The earth is only thousands of years old, as determined by the genealogies in the Bible.	The idea that God created various creatures to replace other creatures that died out over millions of years. Each of the days in Genesis represents a long period of time (day-age view) and the earth is billions of years old.	The idea that there was a long, long time between what happened in Genesis 1:1 and what happened in Genesis 1:2. During this time, the "fossil record" was supposed to have formed, and millions of years of earth history supposedly passed.	The idea that God used the process of evolution over millions of years (involving struggle and death) to bring about what we see today.	The view that there is no God and evolution of all life forms happened by purely naturalistic processes over billions of years.

Any theory that tries to combine the evolutionary time frame with creation presupposes that death entered the world before Adam sinned, which contradicts what God has said in His Word. The view that the earth (and its "fossil record") is hundreds of millions of years old damages the gospel message. God's completed creation was "very good" at the end of the sixth day (Genesis 1:31). Death entered this perfect paradise *after* Adam disobeyed God's command. It was the punishment for Adam's sin (Genesis 2:16–17; 3:19; Romans 5:12–19). Thorns appeared when God cursed the ground because of Adam's sin (Genesis 3:18).

The first animal death occurred when God killed at least one animal, shedding its blood, to make clothes for Adam and Eve (Genesis 3:21). If the earth's "fossil record" (filled with death, disease, and thorns) formed over millions of years before Adam appeared (and before he sinned), then death no longer would be the penalty for sin. Death, the "last enemy" (1 Corinthians 15:26), diseases (such as cancer), and thorns would instead be part of the original creation that God labeled "very good." No, it is clear that the "fossil record" formed some time *after* Adam sinned—not many millions of years before. Most fossils were formed as a result of the worldwide Genesis Flood.

When viewed from a biblical perspective, the scientific evidence clearly supports a recent creation by God, and not naturalistic evolution and millions of years. The volume of evidence supporting the biblical creation account is substantial and cannot be adequately covered in this book. If you would like more information on this topic, please see the resource guide in the appendices. To help get you started, just a few examples of evidence supporting biblical creation are given below:

Evolutionary Myth: Humans have been around for more than one million years.

The Truth: If people have been on earth for a million years, there would be trillions of people on the earth today, even if we allowed for worst-case plagues, natural disasters, etc. The number of people on earth today is about 6.5 billion. If the population had grown at only a 0.01% rate (today's rate is over 1%) over 1 million years, there could be 10^{43} people today (that's a number with 43 zeros after it)! Repopulating the earth after the Flood would only require a population growth rate of 0.5%, half of what it is today.

John D. Morris, *The Young Earth* (Colorado Springs: Creation Life Publishers, 1994), pp. 70–71. See also "Billions of People in Thousands of Years?" at www.answersingenesis.org/go/billions-of-people.

Evolutionary Myth: Man evolved from an ape-like creature.

The Truth: All so-called "missing links" showing human evolution from apes have been shown to be either apes, humans, or deliberate hoaxes. These links remain missing.

Duane T. Gish, *The Amazing Story of Creation from Science and the Bible* (El Cajon: Institute for Creation Research, 1990), pp. 78–83.

Evolutionary Myth: All animals evolved from lower life forms.

The Truth: While Darwin predicted that the fossil record would show numerous transitional fossils, even more than 145 years later, all we have are a handful of disputable examples. For example, there are no fossils showing something that is part way between a dinosaur and a bird. Fossils show that a snail has always been a snail; a squid has always been a squid. God created each animal to reproduce after its kind (Genesis 1:20–25).

Ibid., pp. 36, 53–60.

Evolutionary Myth: Dinosaurs evolved into birds.

The Truth: Flying birds have streamlined bodies, with the weight centralized for balance in flight; hollow bones for lightness, which are also part of their breathing system; powerful muscles for flight; and very sharp vision. And birds have two of the most brilliantly-designed structures in nature—their feathers and special lungs. It is impossible to believe that a reptile could make that many changes over time and still survive.

Gregory Parker et al., *Biology: God's Living Creation* (Pensacola: A Beka Books, 1997), pp. 474–475.

Evolutionary Myth: Thousands of changes over millions of years resulted in the creatures we see today.

The Truth: What is now known about human and animal anatomy shows the body structures, from the cells to systems, to be infinitely more complex than was believed when Darwin published his work in 1859. Many biologists and especially microbiologists are now saying that there is no way these complex structures could have developed by natural processes.

Ibid., pp. 384–385.

Since the evidence does not support their theories, evolutionists are constantly coming up with new ways to try to support what they believe. One of their ideas is called punctuated equilibrium. This theory of evolution says that rapid evolution occurred in small isolated populations, and left no evidence in the fossil record. There is no evidence for this, nor any known mechanism to cause these rapid changes. Rather, it is merely wishful thinking. We need to teach our children the difference between science and wishful thinking.

Despite the claims of many scientists, if you examine the evidence objectively, it is obvious that evolution and millions of years have not been proven. You can be confident that if you teach that what the Bible says is true, you won't go wrong. Instill in your student a confidence in the truth of the Bible in all areas. If scientific thought seems to contradict the Bible, realize that scientists often make mistakes, but God does not lie. At one time scientists believed that the earth was the center of the universe, that living things could spring from non-living things, and that blood-letting was good for the body. All of these were believed to be scientific facts but have since been disproved, but the Word of God remains true. If we use modern "science" to interpret the Bible, what will happen to our faith in God's Word when scientists change their theories yet again?

Integrating the Seven C's

The Seven C's is a framework in which all of history, and the future to come, can be placed. As we go through our daily routines we may not understand how the details of life connect with the truth that we find in the Bible. This is also the case for students. When discussing the importance of the Bible you may find yourself telling students that the Bible is relevant in everyday activities. But how do we help the younger generation see that? The Seven C's are intended to help.

The Seven C's can be used to develop a biblical worldview in students, young or old. Much more than entertaining stories and religious teachings, the Bible has real connections to our everyday life. It may be hard, at first, to see how many connections there are, but with practice, the daily relevance of God's Word will come alive. Let's look at the Seven C's of History and how each can be connected to what the students are learning.

Creation

God perfectly created the heavens, the earth, and all that is in them in six normal-length days around 6,000 years ago.

This teaching is foundational to a biblical worldview and can be put into the context of any subject. In science, the amazing design that we see in nature—whether in the veins of a leaf or the complexity of your hand—is all the handiwork of God. Virtually all of the lessons in *God's Design for Science* can be related to God's creation of the heavens and earth.

Other contexts include:

Natural laws—any discussion of a law of nature naturally leads to God's creative power.

DNA and information—the information in every living thing was created by God's supreme intelligence.

Mathematics—the laws of mathematics reflect the order of the Creator.

Biological diversity—the distinct kinds of animals that we see were created during the Creation Week, not as products of evolution.

Art—the creativity of man is demonstrated through various art forms.

History—all time scales can be compared to the biblical time scale extending back about 6,000 years.

Ecology—God has called mankind to act as stewards over His creation.

Corruption

After God completed His perfect creation, Adam disobeyed God by eating the forbidden fruit. As a result, sin and death entered the world, and the world has been in decay since that time. This point is evident throughout the world that we live in. The struggle for survival in animals, the death of loved ones, and the violence all around us are all examples of the corrupting influence of sin.

Other contexts include:

Genetics—the mutations that lead to diseases, cancer, and variation within populations are the result of corruption.

Biological relationships—predators and parasites result from corruption.

History—wars and struggles between mankind, exemplified in the account of Cain and Abel, are a result of sin.

Catastrophe

God was grieved by the wickedness of mankind and judged this wickedness with a global Flood. The Flood covered the entire surface of the earth and killed all air-breathing creatures that were not aboard the Ark. The eight people and the animals aboard the Ark replenished the earth after God delivered them from the catastrophe.

The catastrophe described in the Bible would naturally leave behind much evidence. The studies of geology and of the biological diversity of animals on the planet are two of the most obvious applications of this event. Much of scientific understanding is based on how a scientist views the events of the Genesis Flood.

Other contexts include:

Biological diversity—all of the birds, mammals, and other air-breathing animals have populated the earth from the original kinds which left the Ark.

Geology—the layers of sedimentary rock seen in road-cuts, canyons, and other geologic features are testaments to the global Flood.

Geography—features like mountains, valleys, and plains were formed as the floodwaters receded.

Physics—rainbows are a perennial sign of God's faithfulness and His pledge to never flood the entire earth again.

Fossils—Most fossils are a result of the Flood rapidly burying plants and animals.

Plate tectonics—the rapid movement of the earth's plates likely accompanied the Flood.

Global warming/Ice Age—both of these items are likely a result of the activity of the Flood. The warming we are experiencing today has been present since the peak of the Ice Age (with variations over time).

Confusion

God commanded Noah and his descendants to spread across the earth. The refusal to obey this command and the building of the tower at Babel caused God to judge this sin. The common language of the people was confused and they spread across the globe as groups with a common language. All people are truly of "one blood" as descendants of Noah and, originally, Adam.

The confusion of the languages led people to scatter across the globe. As people settled in new areas, the traits they carried with them became concentrated in those populations. Traits like dark skin were beneficial in the tropics while other traits benefited populations in northern climates, and distinct people groups, not races, developed.

Other contexts include:

Genetics—the study of human DNA has shown that there is little difference in the genetic makeup of the so-called "races."

Languages—there are about seventy language groups from which all modern languages have developed.

Archaeology—the presence of common building structures, like pyramids, around the world confirms the biblical account.

Literature—recorded and oral records tell of similar events relating to the Flood and the dispersion at Babel.

Christ

God did not leave mankind without a way to be redeemed from its sinful state. The Law was given to Moses to show how far away man is from God's standard of perfection. Rather than the sacrifices, which only covered sins, people needed a Savior to take away their sin. This was accomplished when Jesus Christ came to earth to live a perfect life and, by that obedience, was able to be the sacrifice to satisfy God's wrath for all who believe.

The deity of Christ and the amazing plan that was set forth before the foundation of the earth is the core of Christian doctrine. The earthly life of Jesus was the fulfillment of many prophecies and confirms the truthfulness of the Bible. His miracles and presence in human form demonstrate that God is both intimately concerned with His creation and able to control it in an absolute way.

Other contexts include:

Psychology—popular secular psychology teaches of the inherent goodness of man, but Christ has lived the only perfect life. Mankind needs a Savior to redeem it from its unrighteousness.

Biology—Christ's virgin birth demonstrates God's sovereignty over nature.

Physics—turning the water into wine and the feeding of the five thousand demonstrate Christ's deity and His sovereignty over nature.

History—time is marked (in the western world) based on the birth of Christ despite current efforts to change the meaning.

Art—much art is based on the life of Christ and many of the masters are known for these depictions, whether on canvas or in music.

Cross

Because God is perfectly just and holy, He must punish sin. The sinless life of Jesus Christ was offered as a substitutionary sacrifice for all of those who will repent and put their faith in the Savior. After His death on the Cross, He defeated death by rising on the third day and is now seated at the right hand of God.

The events surrounding the crucifixion and resurrection have a most significant place in the life of Christians.

Though there is no way to scientifically prove the resurrection, there is likewise no way to prove the stories of evolutionary history. These are matters of faith founded in the truth of God's Word and His character. The eyewitness testimony of over 500 people and the written Word of God provide the basis for our belief.

Other contexts include:

Biology—the biological details of the crucifixion can be studied alongside the anatomy of the human body.

History—the use of crucifixion as a method of punishment was short-lived in historical terms and not known at the time it was prophesied.

Art—the crucifixion and resurrection have inspired many wonderful works of art.

Consummation

God, in His great mercy, has promised that He will restore the earth to its original state—a world without death, suffering, war, and disease. The corruption introduced by Adam's sin will be removed. Those who have repented and put their trust in the completed work of Christ on the Cross will experience life in this new heaven and earth. We will be able to enjoy and worship God forever in a perfect place.

This future event is a little more difficult to connect with academic subjects. However, the hope of a life in God's presence and in the absence of sin can be inserted in discussions of human conflict, disease, suffering, and sin in general.

Other contexts include:

History—in discussions of war or human conflict the coming age offers hope.

Biology—the violent struggle for life seen in the predator-prey relationships will no longer taint the earth.

Medicine—while we struggle to find cures for diseases and alleviate the suffering of those enduring the effects of the Curse, we ultimately place our hope in the healing that will come in the eternal state.

The preceding examples are given to provide ideas for integrating the Seven C's of History into a broad range of curriculum activities. We would recommend that you give your students, and yourself, a better understanding of the Seven C's framework by using AiG's *Answers for Kids* curriculum. The first seven lessons of this curriculum cover the Seven C's and will establish a solid understanding of the true history, and future, of the universe. Full lesson plans, activities, and student resources are provided in the curriculum set.

We also offer bookmarks displaying the Seven C's and a wall chart. These can be used as visual cues for the students to help them recall the information and integrate new learning into its proper place in a biblical worldview.

Even if you use other curricula, you can still incorporate the Seven C's teaching into those. Using this approach will help students make firm connections between biblical events and every aspect of the world around them, and they will begin to develop a truly biblical worldview and not just add pieces of the Bible to what they learn in "the real world."

Unit 1
Body Overview

1 The Creation of Life

God created them male and female

Supply list

Paper   Mirror

Colored pencils   Bible

What did we learn?

- On which day of creation did God make man? **On the sixth day.**
- In whose image did God create man? **In God's image.**
- According to Genesis 1:26, over what were man and woman to rule? **Fish, birds, livestock, all the earth, and all the creatures on the earth.**

Taking it further

- Since we are created in God's image, how should we treat our bodies? **We should take care of our bodies and keep them healthy.**

Challenge: Body Systems

- **The 11 systems of the human body include: skeletal, muscular, nervous, digestive, circulatory, respiratory, skin (integumentary), immune, endocrine, excretory, reproductive**
- **Answers to other questions will vary.**

2 Overview of the Human Body

We are fearfully and wonderfully made!

Supply list

Copy of "Body Wheel" (do not copy back to back)

Crayons, colored pencils, or markers

Paper fasteners   Scissors

What did we learn?

- Name as many of the body's systems as you can and describe what each system does. **Answers will vary.**

Taking it further

- Which body systems are used when you walk across a room? **All of them. Your nervous, skeletal and muscular systems help you move. But also, your circulatory system provides oxygen and nutrients to your muscles. Your respiratory and digestive systems are what give your blood the oxygen and nutrients. And finally, your skin is needed to protect you as you walk.**

3 Human Cells, Tissues, & Organs

The building blocks of our bodies

Supply list

Copy of "Body Cells" worksheet

Body Cells worksheet

A. **Nerve cell**
B. **Muscle cell**
C. **White blood cell**
D. **Skin cell**
E. **Red blood cell**
F. **Bone cell**

What did we learn?

- What is the function of each of the following kinds of cells: skin cells, red blood cells, white blood cells, bone cells, nerve cells, and muscle cells? **Skin cells provide protection to seal out harmful substances and seal in moisture. Red blood cells carry oxygen to and carbon dioxide away from all the cells of the body. White blood cells eliminate invading germs and other harmful substances. Bone cells provide strength. Nerve cells relay messages. Muscle cells contract and expand to allow movement.**

Taking it further

- How has God uniquely designed red blood cells to transport oxygen? **They are round and smooth so they easily flow through blood vessels. Also, their cell membranes allow oxygen and carbon dioxide to easily pass through.**

- How are nerve cells specially designed to carry signals? **They have long tendrils or finger-like projections allowing a few cells to cover a large distance in the body, and thus signals can travel very quickly.**

- How did God design skin cells to perform their special functions? **Their rectangular shape allows them to fit snuggly together making an effective wall against germs and preventing moisture loss in your body.**

- With all these cells working together, what do you think is the largest organ in the body? **You might guess the stomach, heart or brain, but your skin is actually the largest organ in your body.**

Challenge: Tissue Types

Skin: **Epithelial tissue**
Muscles: **Muscle tissue**
Tendons: **Connective tissue**
Lining of the mouth: **Epithelial tissue**
Brain: **Nerve tissue**
Inside of lungs: **Epithelial tissue**
Fat: **Connective tissue**
Bones: **Connective tissue**

QUIZ 1 Body Overview

Lessons 1–3

Fill in the blanks with the correct term.

1. Many cells working together are called a _**tissue**_.
2. _ **Red blood**_ cells carry oxygen to the body.
3. _**Muscle**_ cells stretch and contract to allow for movement.
4. The _**cell membrane**_ acts like the skin of a cell.
5. The _**nucleus**_ is the brain or control center of a cell.
6. Vacuoles are where cells store _**food (or other nutrients, or waste)**_.
7. Mitochondria break down food to provide _**energy**_ for the cell.
8. Humans were created in _**God's**_ image.
9. The _**skeletal**_ system provides strength for the body.
10. _**Nerve**_ cells can be over a yard long.

11. Nutrients are provided to the body through the _digestive_ system.

12. _Skin_ protects the body from harmful substances outside the body. **(also accept white blood cells)**

13. _Bone_ cells have a criss-cross shape.

14. Several tissues working together are called an _organ_.

15. A system is made up of _cells, tissues,_ and _organs_ all working together to perform a specific function.

Challenge questions

Fill in the blanks with the correct term.

16. The _endocrine_ system produces chemical messengers to control body functions.

17. Waste products are removed from the body by the _kidneys or excretory system _.

18. A mother carries the unborn baby in her _womb or uterus_.

19. Bones are _connective_ tissue.

20. _Epithelial_ tissue covers the inside of your stomach.

21. Your brain is made up of _nerve_ tissue.

Unit 2
Bones & Muscles

The Skeletal System

Structure and strength

Supply list

Copy of "Sandy Skeleton" (do not copy back to back)

Scissors   5 paper fasteners for each
                            child

Supplies for Challenge

Tape measure

What did we learn?

- What are three jobs that bones perform? **They provide strength, produce blood cells, and store calcium for future use.**
- How are muscles connected to bones? **By cords called tendons.**

- What keeps bones from rubbing against each other at the joints? **A cushioning material called cartilage is between the bones.**
- How many bones does an adult human have? **206.**
- What is the main mineral in bones? **Calcium.**

Taking it further

- What do you think is the largest bone in the body? **The femur or large leg bone is the longest and largest bone in the body.**
- Why does this bone need to be so large? **The femur bones support most of the body's weight.**
- What do you think are the smallest bones in the body? **The three bones in the inner ear—the malleus, incus, and stapes—are the smallest bones.**

Names of Bones

What's a clavicle?

Supply list

Washable gel pens   Anatomy book

Supplies for Challenge

Anatomy book

Copy of "What's My Name?" worksheet

What did we learn?

- Review the names of the bones by pointing to each bone as you name it.

- Is your cranium above or below your mandible? **Your cranium, or skull, is above your mandible, which is your jaw bone. Of course, this is not true if you are standing on your head.**
- What is moving if you wiggle your phalanges? **Your fingers and your toes.**

Taking it further

- What happens if you cross your legs and gently hit just below your patella? **Your leg swings out with a reflex action. We will learn more about this when we study the nervous system.**

- Why do we have Latin names for body parts? **This allows scientists to communicate about the body even if they do not speak the same language. This is why many scientific terms, not just body parts, are in Latin.**

Challenge: What's My Name? worksheet

1. I hold your ribs together. **Sternum.**
2. Your collar rests on me. **Clavicle.**
3. Pat me on the back. **Scapula or vertebrae.**
4. I support your weight when you stand. **Femur.**
5. Listen, you might find us in a blacksmith shop. **Hammer, anvil, and stirrup.**
6. I'm in your leg, and that's no lie. **Fibula.**
7. I rotate around your wrist. **Radius.**
8. You wouldn't want to stub me. **Phalanges.**
9. Man, I talk a lot. **Mandible.**
10. When you cross your legs, I pop up. **Patella.**

Types of Bones

Are all bones created equal?

Supply list

Anatomy book

Model of Sandy Skeleton from lesson 4

Supplies for Challenge

2 chicken leg or thigh bones

Vinegar

Cup

What did we learn?

- Which bones are designed mainly for protection of internal organs? **Flat bones such as your cranium and ribs.**
- Which type of bones helps determine what your face will look like? **Irregular bones in your face.**

- Which type of bones works closely with your circulatory system to replace old blood cells? **The long bones in your arms and legs.**

Taking it further

- Why are the long bones filled with marrow and not solid? **If they were solid, they would be too heavy to move easily. Also, the hollow design gives the bones more strength, since a cylinder is stronger than a solid rod. Finally, the marrow is where the red blood cells are produced.**
- What is the advantage of having so many small bones in your hands? **This allows you to be flexible and move your fingers in lots of different ways so you can scratch your back, pick up a baby or cook dinner.**

Joints

Connections are important

Supply list

Items found around your house

Supplies for Challenge

2 wooden pencils

Wide rubber bands

Tacks

Scavenger Hunt

- door hinges: **Hinge.**
- sliding doors: **Gliding.**
- joints in pets: **Depends on the pet—dogs and cats have many of the same types of joints as humans including ball and socket, hinge, and others.**

- LEGO® pieces: **May be able to find ball and socket, pivot, or saddle joints.**
- nut crackers: **Hinge.**
- pliers: **Pivot.**

What did we learn?

- What was the most common joint found around your house? **You probably found lots of hinges. This is the simplest kind of joint and is actually a modified lever and a very efficient way to move things.**

Taking it further

- Which came first, the joints in the body or the joints in your house? **Obviously, the body was created first. Man realized the beauty and usefulness of God's designs and used them in many of his own inventions.**
- Why do you need so many different kinds of joints in your body? **The different kinds of joints give our bodies lots of flexibility and strength, allowing us to move in so many different ways.**

8 The Muscular System

Making it move

Supplies for Challenge

Piece of raw steak or other meat

Magnifying glass

What did we learn?

- How does a contracted muscle feel? **More rigid than a relaxed muscle.**
- How does a muscle get stretched? **After it relaxes, it is pulled by another muscle attached to the opposite side of a bone.**

Taking it further

- How does a muscle know when to contract? **The brain sends a message to it telling it to contract.**
- How does your face express emotion? **Your brain works together with your muscles to change the expression on your face. Muscles around your mouth and eyes move to show sadness, surprise, anger or happiness.**

9 Different Types of Muscles

Aren't they all the same?

Supply list

Yard stick   Stopwatch

What did we learn?

- What are the two types of muscles? **Voluntary and involuntary.**
- How can we keep our muscles healthy? **By eating healthy foods, exercising, and stretching before you begin exercising.**
- How do your muscles learn? **Your brain automates functions that you do over and over again.**

- What are some advantages of exercising? **Muscle strength, speed, endurance, and more energy.**

Taking it further

- Do you need to exercise your facial muscles? **Yes. Make funny faces at your mom.**

Challenge: Muscle Tissue

Diaphragm: **Striated**

Tongue: **Striated**

Esophagus: **Smooth**

Mother's womb: **Smooth**

Hand muscle: **Striated**

Heart: **Cardiac**

 **10**

Hands & Feet

Special designs from God

Supply list

Pencil   Cup

Paper

Supplies for Challenge

Anatomy book   Drawing materials

What did we learn?

- Which is the most important finger? **The thumb.**
- Why is the thumb so important? **It is needed for grasping almost everything.**

- What are some special features God gave to hands and feet? **They have flexibility because of multiple joints, sensitivity because of a vast array of nerves, special gripping skin, and protective nails.**

Taking it further

- What activities or jobs require special use of the hands? **Musician, artist, and construction worker are just a few of the occupations requiring special use of the hands.**
- What jobs require special use of the feet? **Most athletes, for example soccer players and dancers.**

QUIZ 2

Bones & muscles

Lessons 4–10

Place the letter for the correct bone type next to each description below.

1. _B_ Makes new blood cells
2. _A_ Found in hands and feet
3. _B_ Supports most of your weight
4. _B_ Found in arms and legs
5. _D_ Found in face
6. _C_ Gives protection to organs
7. _D_ Vertebrae
8. _A_ Gives flexibility in hands
9. _C_ Ribs and skull
10. _C_ Shoulder blades

Mark each statement as either True or False.

11. _F_ Muscles stretch and contract individually.
12. _T_ Muscles can be damaged by tearing.
13. _T_ Using muscles makes them stronger.
14. _T_ Approximately 40% of your body weight is from muscles.
15. _F_ What you eat does not affect your bones and muscles.

Challenge questions

Mark each statement as either True or False.

16. _T_ The arm and leg bones are part of the appendicular skeleton.
17. _F_ The axial skeleton primarily provides form and strength.
18. _T_ Blood clotting cells are some of the first cells at the site of a fracture.
19. _F_ Broken bones are usually weaker after they heal than before the break.
20. _T_ It can take weeks for a bone to fully heal.
21. _T_ Joints are designed to keeps bones in place and to move freely.
22. _T_ Individual muscles cells each contract to make a muscle contract.
23. _T_ Muscles help blood move through the body.
24. _F_ The heart is made up of skeletal muscle tissue.
25. _T_ Only hands and feet have friction skin.

Nerves & Senses

11 The Nervous System

Telling your body what to do

Supply list

Copy of "Nervous System Coloring Page"

Stop watch   Ruler

Small object such as an eraser, pebble, or small toy

What did we learn?

- What are the three main parts of the nervous system? **Brain, spinal cord, and nerves.**
- In the response time test, what messages were sent to and from the brain? **The eye saw the object begin to fall and sent that message to the brain. The brain then sent a message to the hand and arm muscles telling them to contract.**

Taking it further

- Name ways that information is collected by your body to be sent to the brain. **Eyes see, ears hear, your tongue tastes, your nose smells, and nerves in your skin send a variety of messages to your brain.**

Challenge: Unique Humans

- Make your own list of things that humans can do that animals cannot do. What accounts for each of these abilities? **Worship God—humans have a soul and animals do not; feel true emotions—this is a complex thing involving the nervous system and the soul; humans train their bodies to do amazing physical feats, animals do not do this, people wear clothing, people are the only creatures that walk completely upright allowing them to freely use their hands—all of these attributes are related to our relationship with God.**

12 The Brain

Captain of the ship

Supply list

3 different colors of modeling clay

Anatomy book

What did we learn?

- What are the three major parts of the brain? **Cerebrum, cerebellum, and brain stem.**
- Which part of the brain controls growth? **Pituitary gland.**

Taking it further

- Which part of the brain would be used for each of the following: running, dilating your eyes, learning your math facts? **The cerebellum controls muscles for running, the brain stem controls pupil dilation, and the cerebrum helps you learn new information like math facts.**
- Is your brain the same thing as your mind? **No, your brain helps you think but your mind is more than just your thinking ability. Your mind is who God has created you to be. It includes your personality, and your soul and spirit, which allow you to have a relationship with**

God. The human soul is what truly sets man apart from the animals.

Challenge: Brain Anatomy

- Thought: **Frontal lobe, front part of cerebrum.**
- Smell: **Sensory area, central part of cerebrum.**
- Heart beat regulation: **Medulla oblongata, part of brain stem.**
- Memory: **Memory center on side of cerebrum as well as hippocampus.**
- Sight: **Visual cortex, at back of cerebrum.**
- Speech: **Speech center behind frontal lobe.**
- Muscle control: **Motor area in center of cerebrum as well as cerebellum.**
- Pupil dilation: **Midbrain, part of the brain stem.**

13 Learning & Thinking

How do you use your brain?

Supply list

6 index cards   6 different colored markers

What did we learn?

- Which part of the brain does each of the following: stores short-term memories, stores long-term memories, controls learning and thinking, controls the senses? **Hippocampus—short-term memory, cerebral cortex—long-term memory, cerebrum—learning/thinking, senses.**
- Which side of the brain controls the left side of the body? **The right side.**
- What is necessary for a healthy brain? **Good nutrition, sleep, and mental exercise.**

Taking it further

- List ways you can learn something. **By hearing, feeling, seeing, doing, smelling, and tasting. You actually will remember something best if you see it, hear it, say it back, and then associate it with something else.**

- What is something you have trouble learning? **Come up with a new way to try to remember it. For example, if you have trouble remembering how to spell a word, write the letters you usually get wrong in a different color to help you see the right way to spell it.**

Challenge: Logic Puzzles

1. **The two 50 pound people go over together. One returns with the boat. One 100 pound person crosses over. The first 50 pound person returns with the boat. Again both 50 pounders cross over and one returns with the boat. The second 100 pound person crosses over. The second 50 pound person returns and picks up the first 50 pound person. This requires the boat to make 9 trips across the river.**

2. **Ask either person, "If I ask the other person which road leads to the nearest town what would he say?" If this is the person that tells the truth, he will tell you the lie the other person would say. If this person is the one that tells a lie, he will tell you a lie even though the other person would have told the truth. Either way, the answer you get will be the wrong road to take so you can take the other road.**

14 Reflexes & Nerves

Faster than lightning

Supply list

2 sharp pencils or 2 toothpicks
Blindfold

Supplies for Challenge

Drawing materials
Research materials on multiple sclerosis

What did we learn?

- How do reflex reactions differ from other nervous system messages? **They only go to the spinal cord not to the brain, so they are much faster.**
- Why do we have reflexes? **They help us avoid dangerous situations.**
- What are some different types of sensations detected by your nerves? **Texture, temperature, pain, vibration, and pressure.**

Taking it further

- What reflexes might you experience? **You duck if you sense something coming at you, close your eyes, or quickly pull back your hand when you touch something hot.**
- How does the sense of touch differ from your fingertips to the back of your arm? **More nerves on the fingers allow you to detect more subtle differences.**
- Why do you need a larger number of nerves on the bottoms of your feet? **To help you detect differences in the walking surface so you can keep your balance and not trip.**

15 The Five Senses

Letting your brain know what's out there

Supply list

3 bowls	Sandwich bag filled with ice
Hot water	Jacket with a zipper
Warm water	2–3 straight pins
Cold water	

Supplies for Challenge

Glue	Paper

What did we learn?

- What are your five senses? **Sight, hearing, taste, smell, and touch.**
- Which of these senses usually gives us the most information? **Sight.**
- How does your brain compensate for the loss of one of your senses? **Your brain uses the other senses more to gather missing information.**

Taking it further

- You have nerves all over your skin, so why don't you feel your clothes all day long? **Since the nerves detect the same feelings all day, your brain learns to ignore those messages so you don't notice your clothes. But if you really concentrate on it, you can feel your shirt rubbing against your arm.**
- Your eyes see your nose all day long. Why don't you notice it all the time? **Since your eyes see your nose in your peripheral vision all the time, your brain learns to ignore that image, and it disappears. If you really try, you can see your nose. Cover one eye, and it will be more obvious.**
- If you are in the hot sun for a while then you go inside, the room feels cold. Why? **Your brain is comparing the new temperature to the old temperature and decides it is cold. But after a few minutes, your brain becomes used to the new temperature and you don't feel cold anymore.**

Challenge: Braille System

- **There are many more nerves in your fingertips than in the other parts of your hand, thus making it easier to feel differnt patterns of bumps.**

16 The Eye

Window to the world

Supply list

Paper tube (such as a paper-towel roll or a rolled piece of paper)

Piece of paper

Supplies for Challenge

Anatomy book

What did we learn?

- Name four important parts of the eye. **Lens, pupil, iris, retina, rods and cones, and optic nerve.**

- How does your brain compensate for different amounts of light in your surroundings? **By opening and closing the pupil—contracting and relaxing the iris.**

- How does your brain help you to focus on items that are near and items that are far away? **By adjusting the shape of the lens—by contracting muscles in the eye.**

- Why did God design our bodies with two eyes instead of just one? **Two eyes at different positions give depth perception. Also, if one eye is damaged the other can compensate.**

- How does having two eyes help with a 3-dimensional image? **Each eye views an object from a different angle allowing you to see more of the sides and giving you a better idea of the whole object.**

- Since you have a blind spot, how can you see what is in that spot? **Your brain fills in with what is around the blind spot.**

Taking it further

- Name some ways that the eye is protected from harm. **Eyelids and eyelashes keep out debris, tears wash away debris, the pupil contracts in bright light, the skull protects the eyes from impact.**

- Why do some people have to wear glasses or contact lenses? **The brain adjusts the lenses in the eyes to bring images into focus. Some people have lenses that are too flat or too round to be changed enough to make the images focus properly. Eyeglasses or contact lenses help compensate for these misshapen lenses in the eyes.**

- Why can you fool your eyes or your brain into thinking you saw something you didn't actually see? **Your brain makes certain assumptions about what it expects to see based on what you normally see. If something is unusual you might be fooled, at least for a little while.**

Challenge: Liquid in Your Eyes

- Lens: **Changes shape to focus on an image.**
- Pupil: **Dilates or closes to control amount of light entering eye.**
- Iris: **Controls size of pupil.**
- Cornea: **Front of the eye—protects lens.**
- Rods: **Detect light.**
- Cones: **Detect color.**
- Retina: **Contains rods and cones, detects image.**
- Optic nerve: **Nerve that transmits image to the brain.**
- Vitreous humor: **Keeps eyeball firm.**
- Aqueous humor: **Keeps front of eye firm, supplies nutrients to front of eye.**

17 The Ear

Do you hear what I hear?

Supply list

Copy of "Do You Hear What I Hear?" worksheet

Do You Hear What I Hear? worksheet

_A_ Steaming tea kettle   _C_ Man singing

_D_ Violin   _B_ Bass drum

_C_ Falling snow   _D_ A TV show
_A_ A jet engine   _B_ A whisper

What did we learn?

- What characteristic of a sound wave determines how high or low a sound will be? **The frequency, or spacing, of the waves determines the pitch.**
- What characteristic of a sound wave determines how loud or soft a sound will be? **The amplitude, or height, of the waves determines the volume.**

Taking it further

- Why do two different instruments playing the same note at the same loudness sound different? **A note played by an instrument is not one single pitch. It actually has the same note played at various intervals called harmonics. For example, a C on the piano will sound** very different than a C on a trumpet because of the different harmonics that are generated by the instrument.

- Name several ways to protect your hearing. **Ear plugs, ear phones, and turning down the volume.**
- How do you suppose deaf children learn to speak? **They watch other people to learn how to move their tongues, mouths and throats. They also can feel air movement from their mouths. Watch your mouth in a mirror as you say the sound of b and p. These sounds look the same. Then feel the air flow from your mouth as you say the same sounds. The p sound pushes out puffs of air but the b sound does not.**
- How do you think a CD player or a telephone makes sounds? **Electronic devices such as telephones and CD players take electrical signals and send them through a device that vibrates, causing the air to move and thus making sounds from the electrical signals. This is the opposite of how your ears work, since your ear takes vibrations and turns them into electrical signals.**

18 Taste & Smell

What's for dinner?

Supply list

Paper towels	Potato
Salt	Apple
Sugar	Carrot

Several spices or other items with familiar smells (cinnamon, peppermint, lemon juice, vinegar)

What did we learn?

- What four flavors can your tongue detect? **Salty, sweet, sour, and bitter (and possibly umami).**
- How does your tongue detect flavors? **Bits of food dissolved in saliva touch different taste buds in your mouth, and the taste buds generate electrical signals that go to the brain.**
- How does your nose detect fragrances? **Scent particles enter your nasal cavity where smell-detecting nerves send signals to your brain.**

Taking it further

- Can you still taste foods when you have a stuffy nose? **Depending on how bad your cold is, you may or may not be able to smell the foods. If your nose is really stuffy,** the foods may taste bland and you may lose some of your appetite.
- Smells are used for more things than just enjoying food. List some other uses for your sense of smell. **Detecting dangerous odors such as smoke or gas, enjoying flowers, smelling the fresh air right after it rains.**
- Oranges and grapefruits are both sweet and sour. Why do they taste different? **They have different proportions of sweet to sour. Also, they have different fragrances. This gives them each a unique flavor.**
- Cocoa is very bitter. Why does chocolate candy taste so delicious? **The sweetness of the sugar combined with the bitterness makes it pleasant.**

Challenge: How We Taste and Smell

- What is the input to each of your senses? **Sight—light/electromagnetic waves; sound—sound waves/mechanical waves/vibrating air; touch—direct stimulation of nerves in the skin; taste—chemicals in food; smell—odorants, which are also chemicals in food or other items.**

Nerves & Senses

Lessons 11–18

1. Name the five senses your brain uses to collect information about the outside world.

Sight	**Taste**	**Touch**
Hearing	**Smell**	

Match each part of the brain with its function.

2. _D_ Cerebellum

3. _F_ Brain stem

4. _E_ Spinal cord

5. _C_ Cerebrum

6. _B_ Hippocampus

7. _A_ Pituitary gland

Mark each statement as either True or False.

8. _T_ You can improve your intelligence by exercising your brain.

9. _T_ Smells can bring back memories.

10. _F_ You don't need to wear a bike helmet when you ride your bike.

11. _F_ The left side of the brain controls the left side of the body.

12. _T_ What you eat affects your brain.

13. _F_ Reflexes are slower than normal signals to the brain.

14. _T_ Your brain fills in for the blind spot in your eye.

15. _T_ The louder the sound is the higher its amplitude.

Challenge questions

Choose the best answer for each question below.

16. _B_ Which nervous system is the only one capable of higher level complex thought?

17. _C_ Which neurons process and generate signals?

18. _A_ What is the function of myelin?

19. _D_ What liquid is found in the middle of the eye?

20. _C_ What part of the ear controls balance?

21. _A_ Which part of the tongue chemically reacts with food molecules?

22. _B_ What kind of molecules produce smells?

Unit 4

Digestion

19 The Digestive System

What happens to my lunch?

Supply list

Sandwich   Clock

Copy of "Where's My Lunch?" worksheet

Supplies for Challenge

Anatomy book

Copy of "Digestive System" worksheet

What did we learn?

- What are the main parts of the digestive system? **Teeth, tongue, esophagus, stomach, small intestine, and large intestine.**
- What role do your teeth play in digestion? **They grind and chop your food into small enough pieces to swallow.**
- What role does your tongue play in digestion? **It helps move the food around in your mouth so you can chew it up, and it helps you swallow the food.**
- Which is longer, your small intestine or your large intestine? **Your small intestine.**
- Which is wider, your small intestine or your large intestine? **Your large intestine.**

Taking it further

- Can you eat or drink while standing on your head? **Yes. You may think that gravity pulls the food into your stomach, but that is not the case. Involuntary muscles inside your esophagus push the food down, so you can swallow even when you are upside down. You can test this by sipping some water through a straw while standing on your head. You may need some help to do this.**
- Why do some foods spend ½ hour in the stomach while other foods spend 3 hours in the stomach? **Foods that are high in fat or protein take longer to break down than foods that are mostly starches.**
- What makes you feel hungry? **When your stomach is empty, or nearly empty, it has nothing to move around, so it sends a message to your brain that you need more food. Only then do you feel hungry.**
- Why did God design your body with a way to make you feel hungry? **Because humans are warm-blooded, they need to have a fairly constant supply of energy to help maintain their body temperature. Also, eating regularly helps us to have the energy necessary to do all the activities we like to do.**

Challenge: Digestive System worksheet

1. _I_ Pancreas
2. _B_ Salivary glands
3. _A_ Tongue
4. _L_ Anus
5. _D_ Esophagus
6. _K_ Small intestine
7. _F_ Stomach
8. _E_ Liver
9. _G_ Gall bladder
10. _H_ Duodenum
11. _C_ Epiglottis
12. _J_ Large intestine

Teeth

Grind that food

Supply list

Tagboard, poster board, or other thick paper

Modeling clay	Scissors
Plaster of Paris	Small bowl or cup
Foil	Spoon
Tape	

Supplies for Challenge

Three colors of modeling clay

What did we learn?

- What is the job of each kind of tooth? **Incisors are for biting and cutting, canines are for tearing, and bicuspids and molars are for grinding.**
- Why do people have baby teeth and why do they fall out? **You need small teeth when your mouth is small. Teeth can't grow like the rest of your body so the small teeth fall out, making room for larger teeth as your mouth gets larger.**

Taking it further

- Why do we need to take care of our teeth? **If you don't take care of them, your teeth can get holes in them (cavities), break, or even fall out making it hard to eat and causing you pain.**

Dental Health

Taking care of those teeth

Supply list

Toothbrush	Dental floss
Toothpaste	Mirror

What did we learn?

- What are three things you can do to have healthy teeth? **Brush regularly, floss regularly, eat healthy foods, and visit the dentist regularly.**
- How does brushing your teeth help keep them healthy? **Brushing removes plaque and reduces the likelihood of getting cavities.**
- List some foods that are good for your teeth. **Fruits, vegetables, and milk.**
- List some foods that are bad for your teeth. **Hard candy, sugary gum, and sipping sweet drinks for a long time.**

Taking it further

- Since your baby teeth are going to fall out anyway, why do you still need to brush them and take care of them? **You need to develop good habits even if you only have baby teeth. You will have a combination of baby and permanent teeth for several years. Also, even if your teeth are not damaged, bacteria can cause damage to the gums if you never clean your teeth.**

22 Nutrition

What should you eat?

Supply list

Foods from all of the food groups
    (including breads/grains, fruits, vegetables, dairy,
    and meat/nuts/dried beans)

Supplies for Challenge

Copy of "Nutrition" worksheet

What did we learn?

- What are the five food groups listed in this lesson? **Breads/grains, fruits, vegetables, dairy products, meat/beans.**

- What types of foods should you eat only a small amount of each day? **Junk foods such as cookies, candy, chips, and soda.**

- Why is variety in your diet important? **Different foods have different nutrients so you should eat a variety in order to get all the different things your body needs.**

Taking it further

- Can a vegetarian eat a balanced diet? Hint: What other foods contain proteins found in meat? **Vegetarians can carefully combine plant products, such as dried beans, legumes, and nuts to obtain the same proteins as in meats.**

- Is it necessary to eat dessert to have a healthy diet? **No, but it depends on what you consider dessert. Pie is not a great choice, but a banana would make a good dessert.**

Challenge: Nutrition worksheet

- **It is likely that the french fries and hamburger will have more calories, fat, and salt than the other foods. Which food is best for you depends on how you define what is good to eat. Fruits and yogurt are generally lower in calories, fat, and salt, so are probably better for you, but spaghetti with tomato sauce can be very healthy as well.**

23 Vitamins & Minerals

Do I have to go to a mine to get minerals?

Supply list

Food in your kitchen   Pencil
Paper

What did we learn?

- What are the three main forms of energy found in food? **Carbohydrates, proteins, and fats.**

- How can we be sure to get enough vitamins and minerals in our diet? **The best way is to eat a variety of foods.**

- Why is water so important to our diet? **Our bodies have a lot of water in them and use water for many different functions. Also, we lose water when we sweat and when we breathe, so we need to replace that water every day.**

Taking it further

- Can you drink soda instead of water? **Soda and other drinks have water in them and the body can use that water. However, too much soda or other sweet drinks can give us more calories than we need. Also, soda may have a lot of salt in it, which can be unhealthy if you have too much. Finally, drinks containing sugar or salt can actually make you thirstier!**

- Are frozen dinners just as healthy as fresh food? **Frozen dinners generally have a lot more fat, salt and calories than their fresh-made counterparts. They may be quicker and easier but they are not necessarily healthier.**

- Is restaurant food as healthy as home-cooked food? **It depends on the restaurant. Some restaurants have salad bars and offer lots of choices for healthy foods. However, much restaurant food, especially fast food, is high in fat and calories, and limited in vegetables and fruits.**

Digestive System

Lessons 19–23

1. Name the six major parts of the digestive system.
   **Teeth   Tongue   Esophagus   Stomach
   Small intestine   Large intestine**

Match the type of tooth with its function.

2. _B_ Incisors

3. _A_ Canines

4. _C_ Bicuspids and Molars

Short answer:

5. Why is it important to take good care of your teeth? **So you don't get cavities or gum disease. To keep your teeth healthy.**

6. How do you take good care of your teeth? **Brush and floss regularly and visit your dentist regularly.**

7. Why is important to eat healthy foods? **To have energy to do the things you want to do and to keep your body healthy.**

8. Name the five different food groups you learned about. **Bread/grains, Fruits, Vegetables, Dairy, Meat/ beans.**

9. Name the three forms of energy in food. **Carbohydrates, proteins, fat.**

10. What two other important types of compounds do we get from our food? **Vitamins and minerals.**

Challenge questions

Mark each statement as either True or False.

11. _T_ Enzymes play a crucial role in digestion.

12. _F_ The gall bladder stores gastric juice.

13. _T_ Pancreatic juice helps break down fats.

14. _T_ Dentine gives the tooth its general size and shape.

15. _F_ Enamel is one of the softest substances in the body.

16. _T_ Orthodontics is the area of dentistry that corrects the alignment of teeth.

17. _T_ A banana has fewer calories than a cup of french fries.

18. _T_ Many diseases can be prevented by eating the right foods.

19. _F_ Rickets can cause bleeding of the gums.

20. _T_ Eating green leafy vegetables can help prevent anemia.

Heart & Lungs

24 The Circulatory System

The transportation highway

Supply list

Stopwatch

What did we learn?

- What are the three main parts of the circulatory system? **Heart, blood, and blood vessels.**
- What are two functions of blood? **Supplying food and oxygen and removing waste products.**
- What are three types of blood vessels? **Veins, arteries, and capillaries**.
- Which blood vessels carry blood away from the heart? **Arteries.**
- Which blood vessels carry blood toward the heart? **Veins.**
- What happens to the blood in the capillaries? **Oxygen leaves the red blood cells and enters the surrounding tissue. Then, carbon dioxide enters the red blood cells to be taken to the lungs.**

Taking it further

- How is the circulatory system like a highway? **Red blood cells are like delivery trucks because they carry oxygen, nutrients and carbon dioxide to various parts of the body. Valves are like traffic signals because they keep blood flowing in the right direction. The oxygen, nutrients, and carbon dioxide are the cargo that gets transported. We will learn in later lessons how white blood cells are like policemen and platelets are like a construction crew.**
- Why is exercise important for your circulatory system? **It strengthens your muscles, including your heart.**
- List two other systems that depend on the circulatory system to function properly. **The digestive and respiratory systems both depend heavily on the circulatory system. Actually, every part of your body depends on the circulatory system.**
- Why does your pulse increase when you exercise? **You need more oxygen when you exercise so your heart beats faster to get your blood moving faster, thus giving your body more oxygen.**

25 The Heart

Master pump

Supply list

Copy of "The Heart" worksheet

Blue and red colored pencils

Supplies for Challenge

Cow's heart (beef heart) or sheep's heart (may be fresh or preserved)

Rubber gloves   Sharp knife or scalpel

Anatomy book or dissection guide

The Heart worksheet

A. **To arms and head**   D. **From lungs**

B. **From arms and head**   E. **From legs and lower body**

C. **To lungs**   F. **To legs and lower body**

What did we learn?

- What are the four chambers of the heart? **Right and left atrium and right and left ventricle.**
- How many times does a blood cell pass through the heart on each trip around the body? **Two times—once before going to the lungs and once when returning from the lungs.**

Taking it further

- What are some things you can do to help your heart stay healthy? **Eat healthy foods, exercise, and don't smoke.**

- Is your heart shaped like a valentine? **No, it is shaped more like a grapefruit about the size of your fist.**
- Does Jesus live in your physical heart? **No. The phrase "ask Jesus into your heart" is not found in the Bible. When a person is saved through repentance and faith, the Spirit of Christ (the Holy Spirit) dwells in his or her heart (Galatians 4:6; Ephesians 3:14–17). However, this "heart" does not refer to the physical organ, but to the "inner man." Jesus cannot live in someone's heart as He is seated at the right hand of the throne of God (Ephesians 1:20; Hebrews 8:1).**

Blood

Delivery trucks and policemen

Supply list

Several chairs

Several children (if available)

Red Hots candies

Red and blue construction paper

Corn syrup

White jelly beans

Candy sprinkles

Supplies for Challenge

Copy of "Blood Types" worksheets 1 & 2

What did we learn?

- What are the four parts of blood and the function of each part? **Plasma transports the blood cells; red blood cells carry oxygen, carbon dioxide, and nutrients; white blood cells fight germs and other foreign substances; and platelets close wounds.**
- What does your body do to help protect itself if you get cut? **Platelets swarm to the cut and make a patch.**
- Do you have more red or white blood cells? **Many times more red blood cells than white blood cells.**

Taking it further

- What are some of the dangers of a serious cut? **You can lose too much blood or get an infection.**

Challenge: Blood Types 1 worksheet

Blood Donors

A	B	AB	O
A	B	AB	A

Blood Recipients

A	B	AB	O
A	B	A	O

Blood Donors

AB	AB		B
			AB
			O

Blood Recipients

O	O		B
			AB
			O

Challenge: Blood Types 2 worksheet

Blood Donors

A+	A-	B+	B-	AB+	AB-	O+	O-
A+	A+	B+	B+	AB+	AB+	A+	A+
AB+	A-	AB+	B-		AB-	B+	A-
	AB+		AB+			AB+	B+
	AB-		AB-			O+	B-
							AB+
							AB-
							O+
							O-

Blood Recipients

A+	A-	B+	B-	AB+	AB-	O+	O-
A+	A-	B+	B-	A+	A-	O+	O-
A-	O-	B-	O-	A-	B-	O-	
O+		O+		B+	AB-		
O-		O-		B-	O-		
				AB+			
				AB-			
				O+			
				O-			

- Which blood type is the universal donor and which is the universal recipient? **O is the universal donor, AB is** the universal recipient. If you include Rh factor, the universal donor is O negative and the universal recipient is AB positive.

The Respiratory System

A breath of fresh air

Supply list

Copy of "The Respiratory System" worksheet

The Respiratory System worksheet

A. **Nasal cavity**   E. **Alveoli**

B. **Throat**   F. **Bronchial tube**

C. **Lung**   G. **Trachea**

D. **Nose**   H. **Diaphragm**

What did we learn?

- Describe the breathing process. **Your diaphragm contracts, expanding the chest cavity. Air fills the lungs and gases are exchanged. Then your diaphragm relaxes and the air exits the lungs.**

- How do the circulatory and respiratory systems work together? **The circulatory system moves the blood around the body. In the lungs, the respiratory system exchanges gases with the blood.**

- Where inside the lungs does the exchange of gases occur? **In the capillaries surrounding the alveoli**

- What are the major parts of the respiratory system? **Nose, nasal passage, throat or pharynx, trachea, bronchi, lungs, alveoli, and diaphragm.**

Taking it further

- How do you suppose your body keeps food from going into your lungs and air from going into your stomach when both enter your body in the back of your throat? **You have a flap of tissue that covers the opening to the trachea when you swallow but opens up when you breathe.**

- How does your respiratory system respond when you exercise? **Your brain senses that you need more oxygen when you are exercising, so it instructs your body to take more breaths. So you breathe faster.**

- How does your respiratory system respond when you are sleeping? **Your brain senses that you need less oxygen when you are asleep than when you are awake, so it instructs your body to take slower deeper breaths than when you are awake.**

The Lungs

Are there balloons inside my chest?

Supply list

Cloth tape measure   Stop watch

1 or more balloons

What did we learn?

- How does your body keep harmful particles from entering your lungs? **Hairs in the nasal passage filter particles, tissues in the throat trap and kill bacteria and bronchial tubes are lined with mucous that traps particles.**

- How are your lungs similar to a balloon? **They both get bigger when filled with air and smaller when the air goes out.**

- How are your lungs different from a balloon? **A balloon is an empty sac; lungs have thousands of tiny sacs at the end of a series of branching pipes.**

Taking it further

- What can you do to keep your lungs healthy? **Exercise, try to avoid being around people who are sick if possible, and don't smoke.**

- If you breathe in oxygen and breathe out carbon dioxide, how can you help someone who is not breathing by breathing into his or her lungs when you do CPR? **Air going into the lungs is about 21% oxygen and 0.04% carbon dioxide. Air exiting the lungs is about 16% oxygen and 4% carbon dioxide. So when you breathe into someone else's lungs there is still quite a bit of oxygen in the air you exhale into their lungs.**

Heart & Lungs

Lessons 24–28

Fill in the blank with the part of blood that does each job below.

1. _**Red blood cells**_ transport oxygen and carbon dioxide.

2. _**White blood cells**_ surround and eliminate germs.

3. _**Plasma**_ carries the cells around the body.

4. _**Platelets**_ repair breaks in the blood vessels.

Match the term with its definition.

5. _**C**_ Diaphragm   9. _**G**_ Trachea

6. _**A**_ Carbon dioxide   10. _**D**_ Lungs

7. _**F**_ Oxygen   11. _**E**_ Alveoli

8. _**B**_ Bronchi

12. List two ways to keep your lungs healthy: **Exercise, don't smoke, and avoid exposure to people who are ill.**

Challenge questions

Short answer:

13. What is the difference between systolic and diastolic blood pressure? **Systolic blood pressure is the pressure in the blood vessels when the heart is contracting, diastolic is the pressure when the heart is resting.**

14. List two ways that a person might lower his/her blood pressure? **Change in diet, exercise, and medication.**

15. Describe how blood moves through the heart. **Blood enters the right atrium then fills the right ventricle. It is then pumped out to the lungs. Blood returning from the lungs enters the left atrium and then fills the left ventricle. It is then pumped out of the heart to the rest of the body.**

16. Which blood type or types can donate to someone with A positive blood? **O positive, A positive, O negative, A negative.**

17. Which blood type or types can someone with A positive blood donate to? **A positive, AB positive.**

18. Explain the difference between external and internal respiration. **External respiration takes place in the lungs, internal respiration takes place between the blood cells and the tissue cells.**

Skin & Immunity

29 The Skin
Keeping your insides in

Supply list
Hand lotion   Mirror

What did we learn?

- What are the purposes of skin? **To protect you from the outside world, to keep your insides in and moist, and to hold the nerves that collect information for your brain.**

- How does skin help you stay healthy? **Primarily, it helps keep out germs.**

- How does skin allow you to move without getting stretched out? **It has elastin; an elastic substance that stretches then returns to its normal shape.**

Taking it further

- Other than skin, in what other ways does your body keep out germs? **Your nose and mouth have mucus and saliva that trap germs. Earwax helps to keep out germs. Hairs in your nose and ears help to keep out foreign objects. Scabs and white blood cells also keep out or get rid of germs.**

- What skin problems might you experience in a dry climate? **Skin can get too dry and crack open, creating painful sores.**

- What skin problems might you experience in a very moist or humid climate? **Your skin might secrete too much oil, causing oily skin. This can lead to acne.**

- What are the dangers of a serious burn? **A serious burn takes away your skin and allows germs in. This can lead to infection and serious illness.**

30 Cross-section of Skin
What's below the surface?

Supply list
Notebook paper

Skin Word Search

F	**E**	**P**	**I**	**D**	**E**	**R**	**M**	**I**	**S**	S	I	D	O	I
S	K	N	E	D	F	T	**F**	**E**	Q	E	R	D	S	J
A	N	I	O	P	R	T	**A**	**L**	P	**D**	**F**	A	L	G
U	E	**S**	**U**	**B**	**C**	**U**	**T**	**A**	**N**	**E**	**O**	**U**	**S**	D
S	T	**K**	F	R	M	S	E	**S**	W	**R**	**L**	K	J	E
F	O	**I**	L	L	M	N	B	**T**	I	**M**	**L**	O	D	R
P	O	**N**	H	H	B	E	R	I	N	**I**	**I**	S	E	V
S	E	**K**	**E**	**R**	**A**	**T**	**I**	**N**	**G**	S	C	A	S	A
V	**G**	C	X	F	**R**	O	U	U	**E**	S	L	F	D	R
Y	**L**	R	I	T	**R**	T	**N**	**E**	**R**	**V**	**E**	**S**	K	R
N	**A**	T	D	G	**I**	B	U	G	**M**	F	K	H	I	L
E	**N**	S	M	I	E	L	K	F	**S**	**W**	**E**	**A**	**T**	D
R	**D**	I	W	**P**	**R**	**O**	**T**	**E**	**C**	**T**	**I**	**O**	**N**	G
A	S	A	R	E	W	**I**	O	P	Y	M	I	T	T	H
G	F	J	K	Y	T	**L**	L	T	O	I	Y	T	E	F

What did we learn?

- What are the three layers of skin? **Epidermis, dermis, and subcutaneous tissue.**

- What is the purpose of the sebaceous gland? **To secrete oil to keep the skin soft and flexible.**

- In which layer are most receptors located? **The dermis.**

Taking it further

- Explain what happens to your skin when you pick up a pin. **Nerves detect the size and shape of the pin and send a message to your brain. Your brain sends a message to your fingers to pick it up. As you pick it up your skin stretches and bends to the shape of the pin.**

- How does your skin help regulate your body temperature? **Your skin secretes sweat when you are hot, which cools your body as it evaporates. Also, blood vessels in your skin get wider when you are hot to allow more heat to reach the surface of your skin. When you are cold, the blood vessels get smaller to help keep heat in. Fat cells in the subcutaneous tissue also help to insulate your body from temperature changes around you.**

31 Fingerprints

You are unique

Supply list

Pencil and paper
Clear tape
Index cards

Supplies for Challenge

Light corn syrup
Red food coloring
Paper
Meter stick
Copy of "Blood Splatter Chart"
Newspaper
White paper
Eyedropper

What did we learn?

- Where can friction skin be found on your body? **On your hands and feet.**

- When are fingerprints formed? **About 3–4 months before birth.**

- What are the three major groups of fingerprints? **Arch, loop, and whorl.**

- Can you identify identical twins by their fingerprints? **Yes, even identical twins have unique fingerprints.**

Taking it further

- What are some circumstances where fingerprints are used? **They are used to identify suspects in a crime, dead bodies, and lost children.**

- Why do prints only occur on the hands and feet? **These are the only areas where friction skin is needed.**

- Do children's fingerprints match their parents' prints? **No, each person has unique prints that do not match either parent.**

32 The Immune System

Keeping you healthy

Supply list

Research materials on allergies, diabetes, and arthritis

Supplies for Challenge

Research materials on vaccines and antibiotics

What did we learn?

- What are the major parts of the immune system? **Skin, lymph, and circulatory systems.**

- What are the two major types of "germs" that make us sick? **Viruses and bacteria**
- How do tears and mucus help fight germs? **Tears break down bacteria; mucus traps them.**

Taking it further

- Why are a fever and a mosquito bite both indications that your immune system is working? **Your brain raises your body temperature in an effort to kill the germs. Swelling around a mosquito bite shows that antibodies are attacking the invading substance.**

33 Genetics

Why you look like you do

Supply list

Copy of "Genetics Quiz"

Supplies for Challenge

DNA model kit (optional but recommended)
Copy of "DNA Puzzle Pieces" (make additional copies for a longer chain)

What did we learn?

- What are genes? **Bits of information contained in each cell that control your physical development and many other things about you.**
- Why do children generally look like their parents? **Because half of the information that determines what a child looks like comes from the biological mother and half comes from the biological father.**

Taking it further

- If parents look very different from each other what will their children look like? **It depends on the dominant genes. Generally, siblings look a lot like each other even if their parents look very different, but they have the potential to look very different. A couple in England had a very interesting family. The mother had very dark skin and the father had very light skin. They had twins and one had very dark skin and one had very light skin. The combinations of our genes make each of us a totally unique individual.**

- In the past evolutionists claimed that man evolved independently in different parts of the world and this is where the races came from. If this were true, how likely would it be that the different races could have children together? **This is very unlikely. God created all humans from one man and woman. More recent genetic testing indicates that all humans share a common ancestor just a few thousand years ago, which supports the teachings of the Bible.**

QUIZ 6

Skin & Immunity

Lessons 29–33

Choose the best answer for each question.

1. _B_ Which of the following is not a part of your skin?
2. _D_ Which cells are found on the outermost part of the epidermis?
3. _C_ Where is friction skin found on your body?
4. _A_ Which of the following is not a function of the skin?
5. _D_ Which people have the same fingerprints?
6. _B_ Which organ provides a barrier against disease?
7. _A_ Which of the following are produced by white blood cells?
8. _C_ Which of the following does not help filter germs from your body?
9. _A_ How are physical traits passed on from parent to child?
10. _C_ Which of the following grows from a follicle?

Challenge questions

Match the term with its definition.

11. _C_ Arrector pili muscles
12. _E_ Vaccination
13. _B_ Albinism
14. _G_ Double helix
15. _F_ DNA
16. _A_ Carotene
17. _D_ Forensic science
18. _I_ Base pair
19. _K_ Thymine
20. _M_ Cytosine
21. _N_ Gene
22. _O_ Chromosome
23. _H_ Dexoyribose
24. _J_ Adenine
25. _L_ Guanine
26. _P_ Mutation

34

Body Poster

Putting it all together

Final Project supply list

Newsprint or other large paper

Markers

Scissors

Tape

Anatomy book

What did we learn?

- Name the eight body systems you have learned about? **Skeletal, muscular, nervous, digestive, circulatory, respiratory, immune, and the skin (integumentary system).**
- How do some of the different systems work together? **The circulatory system works with the respiratory system to bring oxygen to the body. The circulatory system works with the digestive system to bring energy** to the whole body. The skin works with the nervous system to detect what is going on around us. The muscular system moves the skeleton. They all work together.

Taking it further

- What other systems can you think of that are in your body but were not discussed in this book? **Reproductive and excretory systems are a couple that were not covered, as well as the endocrine system. These systems are briefly discussed in the Challenge sections. You can learn more from an anatomy book.**
- How do you see evidence of God the Creator in the design of the human body? **Answers will vary.**

Human Body

Lessons 1–34

Choose the best answer for each question.

1. _A_ Which of the following are the three main types of fingerprints?

2. _C_ What kind of skin is on the palms of your hands and bottoms of your feet?

3. _B_ Which are not found in skin?

4. _B_ Which is determined by genetics?

5. _D_ Your hip is which type of joint?

6. _A_ What causes a muscle to contract?

7. _C_ Which is not a part of the nervous system?

8. _B_ What is the main function of the hippocampus in the brain?

9. _C_ Which should you eat sparingly for good health?

Match the name of the system to its function.

10. _D_ Circulatory system

11. _A_ Digestive system

12. _E_ Skin

13. _F_ Nervous system

14. _B_ Muscular system

15. _G_ Respiratory system

16. _C_ Skeletal system

Mark each statement as either True or False.

17. _T_ Long bones produce red blood cells.

18. _F_ Your funny bone is a bone in your arm.

19. _T_ It is important to drink plenty of water every day.

20. _T_ You will get most of the vitamins you need if you eat a variety of foods.

21. _F_ White blood cells stop a cut from bleeding too much.

22. _T_ A human heart has four chambers.

23. _T_ Your lungs are filled with branching tubes that end in alveoli.

24. _F_ Your brain is the largest organ in your body.

25. _F_ A sick person will get better if some of his blood is let out.

26. _T_ Skin contains pain and temperature receptors.

Challenge questions

Mark each statement as either True or False.

27. _T_ The endocrine system produces hormones.

28. _F_ The excretory system removes nutrients.

29. _T_ The reproduction system was designed to create new life.

30. _F_ Epithelial tissue moves muscles.

31. _T_ Connective tissue holds the body together.

32. _T_ The skeletal system is divided into axial and appendicular parts.

33. _T_ Only humans have the ability to perform complex reasoning.

34. _F_ Cartilage holds bones in place. 35. _F_ Muscles only move bones.

36. _T_ Reflexes are faster than other nervous system responses.

37. _T_ Dendrites receive input.

38. _F_ The Braille alphabet was developed to allow deaf people to communicate.

39. _F_ Rods and cones allow you to eat ice cream.

40. _F_ The cochlea is part of the middle ear.

41. _T_ Enzymes speed up digestion.

Short answer:

42. Name five bones in your body. **Accept reasonable answers.**

43. Name five muscles in your body. **Accept reasonable answers.**

44. Name four functions of the brain. **Controlling the body, moving the body, thinking, remembering, controlling growth, sight, hearing, smelling, tasting, touching.**

45. List the four major blood types. **A, B, AB, O.**

46. Name two diseases caused by poor nutrition. **Scurvy, rickets, goiter, anemia.**

47. Name the three kinds of respiration. **External, internal, cellular.**

48. Name two purposes of melanin. **Protecting skin from ultraviolet light, protecting eyes from ultraviolet light, giving color to eyes, skin, and hair.**

35 Conclusion

Appreciating the human body

Supply list
Bible
Paper
Pencil

Resource Guide

Many of the following titles are available from Answers in Genesis (AnswersBookstore.com).

Suggested Books

Human Anatomy in Full Color from Dover Publications—Highly recommended

Human Anatomy Coloring Book from Dover—Detailed coloring pages

Biology for Every Kid by Janice VanCleave—Many fun activities

Understanding Your Senses by Rebecca Treays—Good pictures and explanations

Body by Design by Dr. Alan Gillen—Basic anatomy and physiology from a creationist viewpoint

God Created the People of the World by Earl and Bonita Snellenberger—An information-packed coloring and sticker book with the biblical history of people and people groups

Suggested Videos

Newton's Workshop by Moody Institute—Excellent Christian science series

The Hearing Ear and the Seeing Eye by Dr. David Menton—Amazing features God created

Fearfully and Wonderfully Made by Dr. David Menton—Discusses the miracle of birth

Field Trip Ideas

- Creation Museum in Petersburg, Kentucky
- Hospital
- Science museum with human body exhibits
- Doctor's Office

Other Ideas

Build a model of the human body. Inexpensive kits are available from the suppliers listed above.

Dissect a sheep's or cow's heart, brain, or eye. Examining animal parts can give a more realistic idea of what is inside the human body.

Creation Science Resources

Answers Book for Kids Four volumes by Ken Ham with Cindy Malott—Answers children's frequently asked questions

The New Answers Books 1–4 by Ken Ham and others—Answers frequently asked questions

Dinosaurs by Design by Duane T. Gish—All about dinosaurs and where they fit into creation

The Amazing Story of Creation by Duane T. Gish—Scientific evidence for the creation story

Creation Science by Felice Gerwitz and Jill Whitlock—Unit study focusing on creation

Creation: Facts of Life by Gary Parker—In-depth comparison of the evidence for creation and evolution

Dinosaurs for Kids by Ken Ham—Learn the true history of dinosaurs

Master Supply List

The following table lists all the supplies used for *God's Design for Life: The Human Body* activities. You will need to look up the individual lessons in the student book to obtain the specific details for the individual activities (such as quantity, color, etc.). The letter *c* denotes that the lesson number refers to the challenge activity. Common supplies such as colored pencils, construction paper, markers, scissors, tape, etc., are not listed.

Supplies needed (see lessons for details)	Lesson
Aluminum foil	20
Anatomy book	5–34
Balloons	1, 28
Bible	1, 35
Candy sprinkles	26
Chicken bones	6c
Cinnamon, peppermint, and other spices	18
Dental floss	21
Dissection kit	25c
DNA model kit (optional)	33c
Eyedropper	31c
Food coloring	31c
Fruits, nuts, and vegetables	18
Gel pens (washable)	5
Gloves (rubber or latex)	25c
Hand lotion	29
Heart (from a cow or sheep)	25c
Index cards	13, 31
Jelly beans (white)	26
Knife or scalpel (very sharp)	25c
Lemon juice	18
Light corn syrup	26, 31c

Supplies needed (see lessons for details)	Lesson
Magnifying glass	8c
Mirror	1, 21, 29
Modeling clay	12, 20
Newsprint (or other large roll of paper)	34
Paper towels	18
Paper fasteners (brads)	2, 4
Plaster of Paris	20
Plastic zipper bags	15
Poster board/tag board	20
Rubber/plastic gloves	25c
Red Hots candies	26
Rubber bands	7c
Ruler	11
Salt	18
Steak (or other meat—raw)	8c
Stopwatch	9, 11, 24, 28
Straight pins	15
Sugar	18
Tacks	7c
Tape measure (cloth—the kind used for sewing)	28
Tape measure (metal)	4c
Toothbrush	21
Toothpaste	21
Toothpicks	14
Vinegar	6c, 18
Wooden pencils	7c
Yard stick/meter stick	9, 31c

Works Cited

"A ,B, Cs of Brain Tumors." http://www.brain-surgery.com/primer.html.

Adams, A. B. *Eternal Quest: The Story of the Great Naturalists*. New York: G.P. Putnam's Sons, 1969.

Collins, David R. *God's Servant at the Battlefield Florence Nightingale*. Milford: Mott Media, 1985.

'Espinasse, M. *Robert Hooke*. Berkeley: University of California Press, 1962.

"Florence Nightingale." http://www.countryjoe.com/nightingale.

Gish, Duane T., Ph.D. *The Amazing Story of Creation From Science and the Bible*. El Cajon: Institute for Creation Research, 1990.

Gish, Duane T., Ph.D. *Dionsaours by Design*. Colorado Springs: Creation-Life Publishers, 1992.

"Gregor Mendel." http://www.accessexcellence.org.

Ham, Ken et al. *The Answers Book*. El Cajon: Master Books, 1992.

Harcup, John W. *Human Anatomy in Full Color*. Mineola: Dover Publications, Inc., 1996.

"How the Immune System Works." http://health.howstuffworks.com/immune-system.htm.

Jefferies, David. *The Human Body*. Huntington Beach: Teacher Created Materials, Inc., 1993.

Koerner, L. *Linnaeus: Nature and Nation*. Cambridge: Harvard University Press, 1999.

Lindroth, S. *The Two Faces of Linnaeus*. Berkeley: University of California Press, 1983.

Mangiardi, John R., and Howard Kane. *History of Brain Surgery*. www.brain-surgery.com.

"Mapping the Motor Cortex." http://www.pbs.org/wgbh/aso/tryit/brain/cortexhistory.html.

Moore, J. A. *Science as a Way of Knowing*. Cambridge: Harvard University Press, 1993.

Morris, John D. *The Young Earth*. Colorado Springs: Master Books, 1994.

Parker, Gregory, and others. *Biology God's Living Creation*. Pensacola: A Beka Books, 1997.

Roehm, Michelle. *Girls Who Rocked the World*. Hillsboro: Beyond Words Publishing, 2000.

Rudwick, M.J. S. *The Meaning of Fossils*. Chicago: University of Chicago Press, 1985.

Schiebinger, L. "The Loves of the Plants." *Scientific American*. February 1996: 110–115.

Steele, DeWitt. *Investigating God's World*. Pensacola: A Beka Books, 1986.

Treays, Rebecca. *Understanding Your Senses*. London: Usborne Publishing, Ltd., 1997.

VanCleave, Janice. *Biology for Every Kid*. New York: John Wiley & Sons, 1990.

VanCleave, Janice. *Plants*. New York: John Wiley & Sons, 1990.

VanderMeer, Ron, and Ad Dudnik. *The Brain Pack*. Datchet: VanderMeer Publishing, 1996.